The
Modern
Mother's
Handbook

The MODERN MOTHER'S Handbook

How to raise a happy, healthy, smart, disciplined and interesting child — starting from birth

Revised Second Edition

By A Modern Old-Fashioned Mom

Bleecker Street Publishing
New York, NY

For My Mother

B. Street Publishing
New York, NY 10014

Contact information:
modernmothershandbook@gmail.com

ISBN: 978-0692416181

Cover design by A. T.

Photograph of the author by M. B.

CONTENTS

PREFACE

This book will be painless.

The same can't be said about having children, because having children takes serious sacrifice. If you are unwilling to sacrifice, then you are not ready to be a mother. Of course, you say? The problem is that many women—and men—don't fully appreciate the amount of time and level of unrelenting devotion needed to accomplish what is undoubtedly the most difficult— and often most thankless—job in the world. As a result, there are two distinct types of mothers: those who sacrifice for their children, and those who make their children sacrifice for them.

Being a good mother starts by actively learning how to become one the moment you discover you're pregnant. Once the baby is born, your very raison d'être is to become the best mom possible. Yes, there's instinct, but that only goes so far. There is no substitute for reading up on the subject, doing research online, speaking to your gynecologist and pediatrician and asking other mothers—including your own, of course—for ideas, guidance and assistance.

That's where this book comes in. I've read dozens of books and articles on motherhood and rearing children. I've observed and spoken to countless mothers, fathers, grandmothers and grandfathers. I've experimented with this and that advice on my own children. And I've kept 10-years' worth of notes that now make up this book, which is simply a no-frills guide to how I figured things out. (I use the pronoun "her" throughout this book, but most of the advice equally applies to raising girls and boys; and I've changed the names of some parents I've singled out to protect the guilty.)

My two daughters are happy, healthy, smart and, for the most part, disciplined. They're also well mannered, fun to be around and enjoy being kids. If that sounds easy, it wasn't. You'd be amazed at how many miserable, weird, always-sick, disobedient, overweight, rude, malnourished, school-hating children there are out there! And if you're not a dedicated and educated parent, that might be the kind of child your flawless baby turns into by the time middle school rolls around. And God help you then.

Fortunately, you have the power to make sure your child grows up just as you always imagined. Parenting doesn't mean giving up all your free time and personal interests. It's about good planning, hard work and making smart decisions.

Naturally, what makes sense for one mother or family may not make sense for another. There are married, single, rich and poor mothers. There are straight, lesbian and bisexual mothers. There are those who have helpful and loving husbands and partners, and those who do not. Some mothers work because they have to for financial reasons, while others have exciting, fulfilling careers and can afford good childcare. Or maybe they're lucky enough to have family members who watch their children for nothing. Many mothers receive no financial help from anyone, and must do everything by themselves. For them, motherhood can be a very hard job indeed.

Like all advice, you need to determine what makes sense for you. And as your baby becomes a toddler and then grows into a child, your parenting will have to evolve, too. Use this book as a guide, and you'll raise a happy, healthy, smart, disciplined and interesting child, often sighing with a fleeting satisfaction of a job well done.

— A Modern Old-Fashioned Mom

ABOUT MYSELF

My story is pretty typical. I grew up with four siblings in a middle-class family in Massachusetts. I was very athletic, and being from a small town, participation in sports was an opportunity for me to meet new people and indulge my competitive spirit. I competed in the Olympic trials at the age of 16 for swimming, and although I didn't make the U.S. Olympic Team that headed to Seoul, my swimming aspirations secured me a full college scholarship at Boston University. After graduating with a master's degree in education, I moved to Los Angeles and worked for print and broadcast media.

While I was living on the west coast, my father became terminally ill with cancer. I moved to New York City where he was being treated to help care for him and to say my goodbyes. In New York, I began working in the publishing industry and sold ad space for various high-profile magazines for four years. Then I moved to the creative side of the business when I was offered an entry-level photo editor position at a fashion and lifestyle publication. I took a major pay cut for that job, but felt so happy about the decision because I was doing something interesting and rewarding, not just earning a paycheck. It was one of the first times I realized how empowering and liberating decision-making could be, even if it meant having to bring the same 'ol chicken salad lunch to work every day.

After meeting my amazing husband, getting married and becoming pregnant, I made another big decision: to become a stay-at-home mother. I never regretted (not seriously, anyway) those seven years caring for my two daughters; but once my second daughter started kindergarten, I re-entered the work force and have been freelancing ever since. I was lucky in the sense that—a few emotional and financial challenges notwithstanding—everything turned out as wonderful as I had hoped, and it's my sincere wish that you and your family have the same rewarding experience.

The
Modern
Mother's
Handbook

AT THE HOSPITAL

Natural or Epidural

I had an epidural for my first child, and missed the window for an epidural when I had my second. Needless to say, the second birth was much more painful and every time I think about the experience, I shudder. All an epidural does is numb the pain, not unlike how Novocain makes that trip to the dentist easier. An epidural not only alleviates the pain of contractions, pushing and the actually birth, but also any stitching that takes place afterward. It's an individual choice, of course, and there is no wrong way to deliver. That said, even though I'd choose an epidural if I were to give birth again, the bragging rights that come with a natural childbirth are undeniable.

Sleep Alone

After your baby is born and the excitement levels off and it comes time for you to get some rest, send your husband home and ask the nurse to have your baby sleep in the nursery. Don't make the mistake of having the baby (or your husband) stay in your room—you need sleep so just relax, recharge and let others do the work overnight. You'll be reunited with your newborn when she needs to be fed. Let your husband go meet his friends for a congratulatory drink with the understanding that he'll bring you a delicious breakfast in the morning. Don't worry too much about anything other than getting physically healthy immediately after giving birth. It's a super-strenuous experience and you'll need to be pampered for a few days. Take advantage of the nurses and allow them to help. They are professional men and women who make a living knowing exactly how to care for a newborn and for you.

Learn From the Nurses

Most hospitals allow only a two-day stay, which is all that's necessary. During that time, the nurses will walk you through the basics of breastfeeding, swaddling, bathing and diaper changing. Ask as many questions as you can and swipe as many supplies as you can get away with. The first 12 hours after your baby is born will find you at once surging with unbridled hormones and then completely exhausted. The nurses are an invaluable font of information for new mothers, so ask a million questions before you go home. Don't forget to leave a big box of candy at the nurses' station before being discharged.

DAY ONE AT HOME

Accept Help

If you're lucky enough to have your mother, sister, friend or baby nurse staying with you the first few days, take full advantage of their presence. Your life is about to consist of interrupted sleep and a crying baby who wants to be fed. So let your mom do as much as possible, including changing diapers and doing laundry. When she's had enough, she'll make up an excuse to go home.

Now, if you don't have anyone helping, that's okay, too. For the first month, caring for your baby is about as difficult as caring for a loaf of bread, once you get into a routine. All she does is eat, poop, cry, sleep and lie there. But gradually the hard work of being a parent starts and it's like being in a canoe going over a waterfall 24 hours a day. Every woman you know who has given birth before you will tell you to nap when your baby is napping. I can't recommend this suggestion enough. For the first few weeks it's fine to stay in your pajamas as long as you want and get to know and become intimately familiar with your newborn. Let visitors stay for only an hour and remind them to wash their hands before holding the baby.

Give Your Baby a Daily Bath

The day you come home from the hospital, give your baby a gentle bath from head to toe in the kitchen sink. She may cry, but nothing comforts a baby like routine, so make it a daily ritual and it'll quickly become a welcome and fun activity. Plus, hello, it's good hygiene. The cheapest and easiest bath aid is the sponge-mattress thingy that fits into the kitchen sink upon which you lay your baby. I found those large plastic tubs that go inside a larger tub cumbersome and, frankly, a waste of money. Your infant will be taking sink baths for months and the oversize sponges do the trick.

Don't Sleep With Your Baby

One of the things you're going to learn as you and your baby grow together is that you need to be strong for your baby, and do things that are right for her, not necessarily for you. This axiom will be put to the test the first night at home with the baby. Should the baby sleep in the same room with you, so you can make sure she is all right? No! Here's why not:

1) Your room is your room and you'll sleep better with the baby just outside the door or in a nearby room within earshot. Babies can be surprisingly noisy even while they are sleeping. All the baby's sleeping sounds—peeps, whimpers and squeaks—are bound to keep you awake.

2) Nothing is going to happen to your baby so long as she is dressed appropriately and nothing else is in her crib that she may get caught up in.

3) When you or your husband gets up to feed the baby, you won't disturb one another. And your husband should definitely be sharing the night-time feedings.
4) A baby who grows up sleeping alone learns to be independent. It's a good idea to start your child off from the get-go understanding that everyone goes to sleep by themselves.
5) Giving your baby the tools to self-sooth at an early age is one of the greatest gifts you'll pass on to her. And when you drop off your child at pre-K and she goes into the classroom without a tantrum (as opposed to that other kid throwing an absolute fit), you'll know why.

Breast Milk or Formula

Breastfeeding is the way to go, period. Studies show that not only does breast milk offer the best nutrition for your baby, but breastfeeding also helps mothers emotionally rebalance after giving birth. However, despite the unquestionable benefits of breastfeeding, there's absolutely nothing wrong with only giving your baby formula, or at least introducing it early on as a supplement to breast milk. In fact, there is serious upside:

1) Your spouse can use formula for night feedings. Dad will love being responsible at night and the bonding a baby

experiences with her father who is feeding her is good stuff.

2) You can leave your baby with a sitter and not worry about feeding.

3) You can give your baby formula that is room temperature. You do not have to ask a waiter to warm up a bottle of formula if you're not in the mood to breastfeed. (Breast milk can also be room temperature, FYI.)

4) If you're dead set against formula, then you'll still want to introduce a bottle (with breast milk) to your baby so she becomes used to it in case you can't feed her for some reason. Or when dad and grandma want to bond with baby by feeding her.

Give Your Baby a Pacifier

Some baby-rearing experts are against pacifiers. Ignore them. Introduce one to your baby as soon as you get home. The trick is knowing when to use it: whenever your baby is tired, cranky in public or upset. When your baby is tired, give her the pacifier to establish it as a sleeping cue. When your baby is cranky in public, break it out to spare everyone your problem. And when your one-year-old trips and seriously scrapes her knee, a pacifier provides comfort.

But, of course, all good things come to an end. So when your child turns two, it'll be time to pull the plug. Tell her a month in advance, and remind her every week. The day before, tell her you'll be taking her out for ice cream to celebrate her becoming a big girl. The next day, take all the pacifiers and tell her that you're sending them to little babies at the hospital who need them. Throw them in the trash and never give her another pacifier. Never! The complaining, if any, will last no more than a couple of days. It may seem heartless at the time to take away something she loves so dearly but the thing to remember in this case is that children are more resilient than we give them credit for. A pacifier is for a baby. When your child turns two she is no longer a baby. Not only is it unsightly to see a child who is too old sucking on a pacifier, your dentist will tell you that even two is too late!

Go Out

The first few days at home you might be inclined to treat your baby like a Fabergé egg. But while she will be tiny and need special care, she's just as ready to go outside as you are. Lightweight and easy to carry, she's the perfect companion for walks and running errands—allowing you to get some fresh air and establish a new daily routine. Going out for a little bit at a time as soon as you can is just what the doctor ordered. It's also a great way to meet other new mothers. Something you'll want to be sure to do sooner rather than later. Being a new mother can be extremely isolating. Chances are there is another woman exactly like you headed to the neighborhood park. Make friends and try not to spend all day, every day alone.

Introduce a Blankie

When your baby is two months, start resting a plain white burp cloth (easy to surreptitiously replace when destroyed or lost) against her cheek whenever she goes to sleep. The cloth, along with the pacifier, will sooth your baby and also act as another sleep cue. Some moms call them blankies, others call them loveys. Whichever name you give it, this small comforting piece of soft cloth will really make a difference in self-soothing. There is something special about the way it will smell to your baby and it's easy for you to carry around in a diaper bag.

Create a Good Sleeping Environment

For the first two months or so, your baby should sleep near your bedroom in a crib or bassinette. But once your parenting confidence grows, start putting her down in her own room, which should be clean, fun and cozy. During naptime, consider putting on a fan and lowering the shade to bring the sleep cues to four: pacifier, blankie, white noise and darkness. Remember, babies should learn early on that it is safe for them to go to sleep on their own in a darkened room. The white noise is something that may help her get a longer rest depending on how much noise there typically is within earshot of her room.

Don't Become Discouraged

If you're lucky or just plain strong, you'll never become discouraged during the first several months of your baby's life. But as you assuredly know, baby blues and post-partum depression are real and serious conditions that afflict thousands of new moms every year. If you think you're suffering from post-partum depression, seek professional help immediately. You will, in the long run, be a much better mom once you've sorted out your feelings and all of the hormones raging through your body.

But even if you don't meet the clinical definition for post-partum depression, you may feel unfamiliar, negative emotions, which will be confounding because you will have expected this time in your life to be joyful. Here's the reality: You have a baby who eats, poops and cries. You're up during the night. You're alone for hours at a stretch. Your hormones are out of whack. You have a new overwhelming responsibility. Never be afraid to talk about any distress with your husband, family, friends or doctor. Remember, you're human and had a completely different life just days before the baby was born. If you feel a little bit of longing for the way things were, don't worry, it's natural.

Lean on Your Husband

You might realize how difficult it is to be home all day with your baby, but chances are your husband doesn't. If you're like most women, you'll be counting the minutes until he comes home so he can help out and end the tedium that sometimes comes with caring for a baby all day. But guess what? He's going to come home late occasionally and he's also going to want to go out with friends. What's a bored and tense mom to do? Communicate and work out an understanding and schedule. There is no better way to show a new father exactly what it is like to care for a newborn than to leave him alone with the baby for an entire day or night. His appreciation of what your life is like will be more empathetic and he'll likely be more aware of how much you do. Dads also need alone time with their baby, too. So ditch the "I'm the mom, I have to be there all of the time" routine and go see a movie and get a mani-pedi.

Make Mom Friends

It's week four and your husband (or partner) is back to work and you're at the park. As mentioned earlier, solitude and isolation can creep up fast, so make friends with other new moms as soon as you can. Not only will you have someone to talk to, you'll have someone to commiserate and compare notes with. And soon enough, gossip with. The camaraderie with new mothers is very powerful and to this day some of my closest girlfriends are those women whom I met in the park when my first child was a baby.

Be Present With Your Baby

Huh? This advice might sound eye-rollingly obvious, but many new moms equate *being* with their baby with being *present* with their baby. They are two completely different things. Being present with your baby (or toddler or eight-year-old) means getting down on the floor and *interacting* with her. Singing to her, reading to her, tickling her, talking with her. Drawing the outline of her hand on paper. Propping her up on your hip when you're cooking and letting her taste a fingertip's worth of soup. This is more difficult than you think especially if you are tired or just plain bored.

The fact that your baby is in a room while you're on the phone, the computer or otherwise occupied does not at all constitute that wonderful togetherness that your child craves and needs. More than anything else, being present and engaged with your baby for hours a day is the real investment that will pay off in the form of a close, loving and lasting relationship. Why do some teenagers get along with and obey their parents while so many others do not? Because good kids are raised by mothers who do the everyday important stuff. If you're going to take on the job of being the best mom you can, this is an important bit of advice to heed. The days go by very slowly when you are a new mother but the years slip by fast. Take the time now to invest in your relationship with your baby because you won't get a second chance.

Ignore Your Baby

Yes, you must be present with your baby, but that's not enough., It's important, especially for first-time moms, to not overindulge your baby or she will become accustomed to *constant* attention. (Imagine trying to drive somewhere while your five-month-old is screaming bloody murder in the back seat because you're not back there, too.)

Let other people hold your baby and don't run to her immediately every time she cries. Of course, some babies are just naturally better behaved than others, but be hyper-cognizant of the fact that babies and children love nothing more than getting what they want. And they learn the art of manipulation at an astoundingly early age. Once you've spent time with her playing her games, it's ok to ignore her while taking a shower or making dinner. Just be sure to place her in a safe environment for the short time that you are gone and let her cry if she wants to. I always tried to remind myself that all a baby can do to communicate is to cry. So if you run to her every time she cries, she'll only learn to cry that much more.

Read to Your Baby Every Night

When you put your baby to bed for the night, read her a book before turning out the light. Read her a book every single night starting from when she's just weeks old, and don't stop reading until she asks you to stop. Numerous studies show that not only do children become better readers if read to at an early age, but also that the sound of a parent's voice reading out loud to a child is very comforting.

Life goes by fast, and reading together every night is a sweet way to slow life down for you and your child.

Consider Being a Stay-at-Home Mom

Okay, the three-month mark is fast approaching and, if you're on maternity leave, it's almost time to go back to work. Or is it? I'm aware of the difficulty and angst that surrounds making this life-altering decision. I had both a very successful career and a job I loved by the time my daughter was born, but I wanted to be a full-time mom. I was a stay-at-home mom for seven years, until my youngest started kindergarten, at which time I went back to work part-time.

Those seven years were tough and money was super tight, but I wanted to *raise my own children*, and strongly believe that my family will forever be better for it. Of course, many women can't stay home for economic reasons, and many others don't want to because their careers are so fulfilling and they're good at it.

The decision about what to do is a personal one, of course. I've known perfect traffic kids raised by nannies who do all the work while their stay-at-home mom goes to lunch or shops. Same goes for kids raised in daycare while their mothers worked.

But stay-at-home moms automatically avoid many of the problems that sometimes beset nanny-raised children. The most important thing is for you to do whatever will make you happiest, because a happy mother trumps being a miserable stay-at-home mom.

FOUR-MONTH MARK

Sleep-Train Your Baby or Go Insane

Yes, if you don't resolve to properly sleep-train your baby at four or five months, bedtime may become a daily battle that will consume your evenings for years to come and impact many aspects of your family's life. Luckily, sleep-training is easy to do. Initially, no baby is on any kind of sleep schedule—unless you've got that one in a million—so you'll just have to roll with her sleep routine at first. Then, sometime after the four-month mark, it's go-time and here's what you'll need to do:

1) Feed the baby, make sure her diaper is clean and put her in her crib with the pacifier and burp cloth at 6:30 p.m. sharp. (She'll still be taking a few naps during the day.) Read a book to her, give her a kiss, and then close the door and ignore any crying until she's asleep—a process that could take around 30 minutes, depending on how much God loves you.

2) Before you go to bed—say around 10:30 or 11:00—feed her (this would be a good time to use a bottle), change her diaper and leave for the night.

3) When she wakes up around 5:30 a.m. or so, change her diaper, feed her and then leave the room ASAP until she cries again, 7:30 if you're lucky. This last step is crucial.

Don't mistake the first morning waking time (5:30) as her final wake time. Now, she may or may not go back to sleep, but if she doesn't, she should be able to stay in her crib without attention and self-sooth. Do your best to help her stay alone and content (with plush toys or a mobile hanging over the crib) for another 90 minutes or else you'll be getting up at 5:30 for the next four years. Be sure there are a few extra pacifiers in the crib for her to reach in case one falls out during the night.

4) Repeat this routine for several more days and your baby should then easily go to sleep from 7 p.m. to 7 a.m. (though she'll still need that 11 p.m. and 5:30 a.m. visit and feeding for a long while). Needless to say, results may vary!

It's important to remember that babies on proper sleeping schedules sleep better and longer, which helps them to be healthy, happy and secure. Sleep begets sleep. What's more, a schedule will make it easier for you and your husband and your babysitter, which will give you more peace of mind when you're enjoying an evening out together. If your baby is asleep at 7 p.m., then all the babysitter has to do is take care of the 11 p.m. feeding (with a bottle of breast milk or formula) and diaper change. And, setting a 7 p.m. to 7 a.m. sleep schedule will make all the difference in the world when school eventually rolls around.

There are a million studies out there that prove sleep-deprived children do not perform well in school. When you are sleep-training your four-month-old baby, you may not be thinking that what you're doing will have an impact in the long run but I promise you that it does. I have many mom friends who never took this vital step to sleep-train early and they've regretted it for years afterwards. It is one of the rearing-defining differences between the sure-footed and the rookies. Don't make the common mistakes of going into your baby's room to cuddle with her each time she may cry out in the night or allowing your baby to get up constantly in the night to eat (after four months she will certainly not need it unless there is a growth issue that you and your pediatrician have discussed) or come into your bed which will become a very difficult habit to break.

Don't Inflict Your Baby on Other People

True story: Dan and Judy didn't sleep-train their baby, and typically put her down for the night around 9 p.m. or later. One evening, Dan and Judy were invited to an adult party, and brought their baby because they didn't know what else to do with her—why they didn't just hire a babysitter, I'll never know. Anyway, the baby was passed around from one adult to another for a couple of hours while the parents did what everyone else wanted to do, namely to have a drink, have an adult conversation, or anything else except deal with a baby.

To recap: a baby needs to go to bed at a decent hour, period. There's a time and place for babies, and a party after 8 p.m. is most definitely not one of them. Nobody wants to meet or hold your baby at a party, no matter how much they pretend to be enjoying it. Not only is it inappropriate to keep a small baby awake in a loud setting late at night, it's irresponsible, too. So get a clue—and a reliable babysitter!

Hire Some Help

Once you and your baby are in a good routine, seriously consider hiring a regular babysitter two or three times a week during the day to take over for a few hours. Whether it's to go grocery shopping, visit a doctor, meet a friend for lunch or get a manicure, you definitely need alone time to get things done and keep your sanity. So hire someone—high school and college students are good candidates—or arrange a regular babysitting swap with fellow moms and you'll make your life a whole lot better. Always try to remember that there is little place for guilt in child rearing. You're human with natural tendencies to want to do things for yourself and by yourself. Once you find someone who you feel comfortable leaving your baby with, it's also a wonderful teaching experience for her that you leave and always come back! Leaving her for a little while at a time when she's young will only help with kindergarten drop-off years later.

SIX-MONTH MARK

Stop or Continue Breastfeeding

When to stop breastfeeding is solely up to you and your spouse, but try to make it to at least the six-month mark, when your baby will be ready for formula. Your whole job as a mom is to prepare your child for the world, and that means instilling a sense of independence at every meaningful opportunity. Nine months? A year? It's up to you, and while you may naturally enjoy the breastfeeding experience, make sure you don't unnecessarily perpetuate your role as your baby's sole means of sustenance.

Feed Your Baby Real Food

Ever notice how so many parents only order chicken fingers and fries for their children at restaurants? It's because they failed, in an epic way, to properly introduce delicious, nutritional food to their child early on. It's a pain to do, but that's your job, mom! You should start introducing soft solids to your baby at around nine months. Jarred organic food is okay, but you should endeavor to mash up or blend some of what you had for lunch or dinner for her at least once a day.

A baby will eat scrambled eggs, rice, avocado, strawberries, mashed peas, banana, pasta or whatever else you put in her mouth. So try giving her tiny spoonfuls of homemade food whenever you can, following your pediatrician's timetable for introducing each food into the baby's diet, being mindful of possible allergies. Not only is real food more nutritious, but she will also enjoy a wider variety of food as the days go by.

Food Do's and Don'ts

• Once your baby is nine months old, she can practically eat any food you eat (check with your pediatrician for guidance).

• Avoid giving your baby processed food.

• Don't get stressed out about eating. If you feed your baby healthful food, she will grow up eating and loving food that's good for her.

• Only give your children organic milk that isn't filled with hormones, which can bring on early puberty and cause other health issues. There is research coming out practically every day about the dangers of non-organic food, so educate yourself for the sake of your child's health.

• As a rule, it takes three times for a baby to get used to the taste of a new food. So if she spits out those mashed turnips with butter, try, try again.

• The aforementioned notwithstanding, there will be some foods your child will simply not like. Don't force her to eat them.

• Once your toddler is able to talk, make sure she knows she has to always finish her meal. The trick is to give her small portions, and if she is really having difficulty, divide the portion into two and tell her she only has to eat half.

• The time to insist your child finish her meal is at home, not at a restaurant or holiday dinner with family. Nobody needs the aggravation, so don't cause any.

• Teach your child good table manners, which means learning how to hold and use a knife and fork, saying please and thank you, chewing with her mouth closed, asking to be excused from the table when finished, and clearing her plate.

• If you give your child the same breakfast, lunch and dinner every day (because you know she will eat it), then she will become an entrenched bad eater. Mix up her diet daily, or else taste the pain later on.

• Don't make the mistake of always giving your baby or toddler juice. Juice has loads of sugar and all it really does is fill up her stomach and prevents her from eating a nutritious meal.

• Regularly give your baby/toddler/child fruit and introduce them to snacks like carrots, cucumber, hummus and yogurt.

• Let your child order for herself at restaurants.

• If you give your child any kind of unhealthy snacks and junk food on a regular basis, you're a lazy mother and your child is in danger of gaining too much weight and even developing serious diseases later on in life.

• Avoid using food as a bribe or punishment. Ice cream as a reward is a different story.

Say No to Sugar

Speaking of food, there's a new epidemic in the U.S. and it tastes delicious. Some 80 percent of all foods sold in America contain added sugar, which is the main contributor to obesity and childhood diabetes. I'm not saying you shouldn't indulge your child with the occasional multi-colored cereal/popsicle/candy treat, but you shouldn't let them drink soda or sports drinks.

Added sugar is an ingredient in all kinds of foods—bread, yogurt, snacks—even those that bill themselves as "healthy," "all natural," "low fat," and "organic," and market themselves to children. It's a disgrace, and your only defense is to get educated on the subject and always check labels before buying.

TODDLERDOM

Talk to Your Child

Talk to your child. What does that mean? Well, it means everything, and it's the difference between having a wonderful relationship with your child, and a not so wonderful relationship. For starters, it means don't yell at your baby, and don't yell at your child. As a former boss once said to me, "If you have to yell, then it means you don't know how to communicate."

Once your child can speak, drop the exaggerated baby talk and start conversing with her in a friendly, warm and matter-of-fact manner: "Do you want toast or cereal for breakfast?" It also means that when you get frustrated with your child's behavior, talk to her about it: "Listen, I've told you that when I say it's time to go to bed, it's time to go to bed. We've had a long day. We went to the park, we had lunch, we drew together, we danced to your favorite songs and I even let you call grandma. It's time to go to bed. If you don't, then we're not going to do any of those things tomorrow."

It's understandable to sometimes get frustrated and lose your cool, but 99.9 percent of the time when you're frustrated, you should communicate in a calm-ish, reasoned and understanding tone, adding a touch of privilege if necessary. Talking to your child also means discussing the day's plans, asking her questions and telling her about what's going on in your life. And talking also means asking her if she's happy in school, caring about her interests and explaining how the world works.

Think Like an Old Italian Lady

When I was eight months pregnant, my Italian grandmother told me in her broken English how to maintain my household in the presence of a toddler. "She-a touch the vase? You say-a 'No!' She-a climb on the table? You say-a 'No!' You don't put away-a nothing, you-a teach them okay, not okay." And so, I decided to skip installing safety locks all over my house and left the many tempting bottles of wine in my wine rack. I simply told my daughter "No!" every time she tried to do whatever it was she wasn't supposed to do. And when she started to jump on the couch or the bed, I reminded her that she was in her house, not the playground. Of course, you can *never* take your eyes off a child when she's outside, and when they are left alone in a room, that room has to be safe in every sense of the word.

Teaching acceptable behavior and respect for property will also let her know she can't indulge her every whim. So many parents make the mistake of allowing their children to more or less do whatever they want and basically rule the roost. (Saying "Okay" is a lot easier than saying "No" and dealing with the consequences, after all.) I can't tell you how many houses I've been to where there are crayon marks on the walls, stained

26

furniture and toys strewn all over the place. I understand that accidents and mistakes happen, but it's your job to teach your child right from wrong, good from bad and the importance of cleaning up.

When you instill a sense of respect in your toddler, those things she'll be expected to do later at school, like putting all toys away at the end of recess or being quiet while others are talking, will come that much easier to her.

Eat With Your Children

Breakfast, lunch and dinner means super-important family time. Even if you're not eating, you have to sit with your baby or child when she's eating and talk to her. Letting your child eat her breakfast, lunch or dinner while you check your phone or clean up is one of the worst mistakes a mom can make. If you can't understand why you should be sitting with your child and interacting and talking to her when she eats (I understand that her and your meal times may be different), then you're not getting it. Turn the television off, put the phone down, and eat with—or at least sit with— and talk to your child during meals.

As your child gets older, eating meals together will become more and more important. Numerous studies show that children who eat regular family dinners with their parents stay off drugs, make better life decisions and perform better in school. Not to mention when your middle schooler drops those juicy gossip bombs over the dinner table because she knows it's a safe place to talk, you'll be glad you set this precedent early.

Realize That Things Happen in Phases

Why is she getting out of bed at 3 a.m.? Why does she throw tantrums at the park? Why won't she eat raisins anymore? All new parents find out the hard way that sometimes children will start acting differently seemingly overnight, throwing a monkey wrench into the works. Why? Don't ask why, just accept it as a fact. The best you can do is to stay calm and manage the situation as best you can until it resolves itself.

When my youngest daughter was two years old, she started waking up at 10 p.m. for no apparent reason, and she simply wouldn't go back to bed. So I would bring her into the living room and watch a low-volume cartoon with her for 15 minutes and then put her back to bed. After three weeks, she stopped waking up. My point is, try straightforward solutions and know that things will always get better with patient effort.

If a phase lasts longer than a few weeks, ask your pediatrician for advice. Also, don't forget to check in with your mom and ask if she remembers anything resembling what your child is going through. Talk to your mom friends, too. If someone else's child is going through the same kind of phase will make you say, *phew*!

Toilet Training

At around 22 months, it could be time to take that diaper off and cross your fingers. When to do it exactly depends on the child: My eldest daughter wasn't ready until 26 months and it took her several weeks to get used to doing her business in the bathroom, and even then she had to wear pull-ups at night for another six months. My younger daughter, perhaps motivated by wanting to be more like her big sister, was ready at 22 months and was toilet trained in a matter of weeks.

If you're lucky, it'll be a warm time of year and you can be with your child outside during those first precarious days, when accidents will definitely happen. Having the utmost patience is key here. You never, ever want to make your child feel embarrassed in any way throughout this process. Learning to go No. 2 in the toilet is one of the last things a small child feels in control of and it is a big step toward her independence.

Just remember that once your toddler is toilet trained she can no longer go whenever she wants, so always encourage her to go to the bathroom before leaving the house, and plan your day accordingly!

Buy Basic Toys

The must-have toys for girls and boys are Crayons and markers, dolls, and arts and crafts, Legos, cars and wooden blocks. Supplement these with the occasional board game or new toy and your child should never be bored. Kids lose interest in most toys very quickly, so don't overload your house with unnecessary future-landfill. And after your child plays with a toy, make sure she puts it away every single time. Learning to clean up after yourself is an important lesson, and you have enough cleaning to do as it is.

You will come across many new-fangled toys on the market promising to teach your child to read and write when they're three or become the next Mozart. However, I strongly believe that reading to your child will provide more educational stimulation than any toy, so load up on the books. When her birthday or a holiday rolls around and family members ask for present suggestions, always include new books on the list. The luckiest of children are those with an ever-growing library of interesting, age-appropriate books on hand at all times.

Teach a Little Selfishness

You'll see it a million times on play dates and at the park. Your child will be playing with some toy and another toddler will come over and try to swipe it. Many mothers—especially if other mothers are around—will prompt their child to give up the toy in the name of sharing. But that's the wrong message to send. Tell the other girl that your daughter will give up the toy when she's finished with it. A child can't understand sharing if she doesn't first understand the concept of possession. You will also teach both children to wait their turn and be considerate of one another. Once your child has played with the toy for a fair amount of time, you can then tell her it's time to share and move on.

If you get a tantrum, keep your cool and practice the art of distraction. A child who feels frustrated about sharing or lashes out at a friend on the playground is probably going through a very normal developmental stage. And while it's impossible to predict what will cause a tantrum, learning to anticipate and avoid meltdowns will help you avoid some of the stresses that drive new moms to the brink. If you're wondering how? Start this book again from the beginning—you must not have been paying attention.

Play Music

Singing to your baby will come naturally, but don't stop there: Go online and buy some good children's music. My father used to play Woody Guthrie's *Nursery Days* for us all the time, and it's since become a favorite of my children. There's a ton of fun and fabulous music out there in every genre imaginable, so get some, play it often and sing and dance along with your child.

Make Family Albums

In today's world where smartphones are capturing every moment of every day, digital pictures add up at an alarming rate.

But how often do you look at them after a week has passed? Since I cherish pictures from my own childhood and have an appreciation for old-fashioned family photo albums, I started to create one every year after our first daughter was born. Organizing an annual album may seem overwhelming, but doing so on rainy days with nothing else on the calendar is an enjoyable way to spend an afternoon (perhaps with your child). As you go through your endless scroll of photos, you'll be reminded of many happy memories and be forced to select those super special moments that just have to be printed and placed in an album. (You can buy cute, durable and inexpensive albums anywhere these days.) To properly save each moment for posterity, write a short sentence that explains the photo under each one. Besides the fact that you and your family will enjoy looking at the albums for years to come, you'll be surprised how quiet they can keep a nine-year-old when you need 20 minutes to finish dinner.

Put Your Husband in Charge on Weekends

If you're a stay-at-home mom, and even if you're not, you're going to need a break come Saturday morning. So who is going to make a fun family breakfast and get the kids dressed after cartoons? Your husband. Then kick him and the kids out the door so they can go to the park, museum, birthday party, meatball-making class, baseball game or whatever else it is your husband has planned to keep his children entertained. Not all day Saturday and Sunday, just a few hours each day so they can bond and you can relax or catch up on other stuff. (One of the wonderful things my husband always endeavored to do with our daughters on weekends was to introduce different foods to them on their rambles: falafels, Italian subs with roasted peppers, sushi, tacos, Chinese food, fish 'n' chips, miso ramen—you name it.)

Invariably, you'll have to, and want to, be a part of the weekend activities. The point here is to make sure your husband pulls his weight and spends time with his children *doing something*. What's more, many studies highlight exactly how important an attentive father is to the long-term health of his children. Among other things, a strong paternal presence has been shown to boost a child's self-confidence, reduce the risk of mental illness later in life and make it less likely for girls to engage in risky activity.

Don't Do Drugs

Here's a bit of advice that may seem ridiculous, but I've known more than a few moms who think it's okay to have a couple of drinks or smoke pot during the day while watching their children. And I know other moms who openly pop prescription pills and joke about it as if it's something that's just done and accepted these days. Unless you have a serious medical condition that necessitates taking medication, do not venture down this very slippery slope. You can't be a good mom when you're in an altered state.

AROUND THREE YEARS OLD

Be Tough on Your Kids

Whether you have a boy or a girl, you'll likely become intimately familiar with *Dora the Explorer* and/or *Thomas the Tank Engine*. The primary point of those programs is to show why it's always good to be helpful, hardworking and conscientious. My Italian grandmother also frequently told me about how her mother doted on and spoiled her three boys, and cracked the whip on her and her two sisters. Well, the boys grew up to be hapless on every level while all three girls grew up to be hardworking, loving and grounded. I've seen mothers coddle their children to the point of no return, and I've seen fathers think that every little mistake or mishap needs to be a life lesson. You and your husband will need to figure out the right carrot-stick balance, but the goal is to provide loving guidance.

As parents, it's easy to forget that we are not meant to be friends with our children. They need to and want to trust us completely, and that comes with providing stability and setting boundaries. Always be in charge of your toddler—trust me, it's what she needs most. It is usually the child who was not taught early on about who's in charge who has the toughest time adjusting to school. Don't let her run the show or by the time she gets to high school you'll have zero control. Once she accepts that you're always there to guide her to make good decisions

35

she'll also understand that the best part of making mistakes is to learn from them. When she gets older and has questions about the tough stuff, she'll naturally turn to the stalwart and loving authoritative figure in her life—you.

Follow Through With Consequences

Once your child can walk and communicate, it's time to introduce the concept of consequences. If she does something naughty, explain why it's naughty—quickly, don't lecture—and ask her not to do it again. If she does it again, she gets a warning that she'll go into a timeout. She does it a third time, and she goes into a corner out of sight—one minute for every year old she is. If she won't stay in the corner, you put her back until she does. The number-one mistake parents make with threats is to not follow through. Follow through, follow through, follow through! As I mentioned, children feel more secure knowing their boundaries, so do what you say or you'll raise a child who a) will challenge you at every turn, b) won't respect you and c) will get into more and more trouble.

Count to Three

If your child won't brush her teeth, stop complaining or clean up her room, tell her that she has three seconds to comply before she goes into a time out. The first few times you may actually get to three and have to actually put your child into a time out. But soon enough, a stern look and the number two will provide the necessary motivation. Call it magic but there is something about that one-two-three count that works every time!

Brush Things Off

As the parent, it's obviously your job to teach your child everything from how to brush her teeth to distinguishing right from wrong. Sometimes you'll feel like all you're doing is telling her to do this and not to do that. You'll often wonder if any of it is sinking in and if she'll ever be able to venture out of the house on her own. But remember, you're running a household, not the Gestapo, and having fun is more important than making everything perfect. So if she throws a fit, uses a naughty word or draws on the wall, sometimes a laugh and a hug is the proper reprimand.

A we're-all-in-this-together attitude can help in these situations, too. Sometimes when I really lost my temper with my daughter, I would look to the sky and clasp my hands together as if praying to the heavens to give me the patience to carry on. For some reason, this often worked in getting her to recognize that I am human, too. Showing your child that you also need help from her to get through the day can empower her to be considerate.

Never Ban Television

Take away dessert, take away video games, take away toys, but never take away television as punishment. Take my word for it, you're going to need television to keep your child occupied sometimes, and the last thing you ever want is to not have TV as an option. I let my children watch about an hour of television a day. I never felt guilty about it either. As long as you and she are picking educational shows like *Sid the Science Kid* or *Bob the Builder* with positive messaging, it's all good. Everyone needs to tune in and tune out from time to time and watching TV is a great way to do just that for parents and children alike.

Don't confuse watching TV with handing your toddler an iPhone or iPad to occupy her time. Many studies prove that video games stimulate a different area of the brain than TV and allowing your daughter to stare at a screen playing video games for an hour a day is an absolute no-no.

Make Cookies

Of the many activities you can share with your child, cooking and baking should be a regular occurrence. Making a batch of cookies will make her feel useful and close to you, teach her a skill, show her that there's nothing more important in the world than being together, and that it's the little things in life that are the most special. Graduate to making healthy dinners together and she'll be set for life.

Children who help prepare and cook dinner will also be much more willing to try whatever it is they made, too. So, let her come with you to the grocery store, recipe in hand, shop for the dinner's ingredients and get cooking! There are many easy foods your toddler can help with like applesauce and pesto and you just may instill in her the confidence and desire to be a lifelong chef.

Wash Hands

So many mothers I know are constantly taking their children to the doctor's office or emergency room. Not me. The single most important thing you can do to prevent your child from getting sick is to teach her to always wash her hands as soon as she comes home. (Keeping a clean and tidy home helps big time too, but that's another book.) This kind of little habit takes time before it becomes automatic, but you asked for this job. Have her take her shoes off at the door, too.

Keep Your Sick Kid at Home

If you follow the rule about always washing hands and eating healthfully, your child will not get sick very often. But when she does, keep her home and away from other children. If that means you miss a dinner or an outing with another family, so be it. There's nothing worse than a Typhoid Mary mom. Allowing a child to get the rest she needs to recuperate is something parents can very easily overlook.

Give Your Child Options

From the moment your baby is born, she has free will like you do. A very common mistake many parents make is to not give their child choices. You don't have to offer choices all the time, of course, but when your child is resisting an idea, like not wanting to do a certain activity or not wanting to play a sport, then give her two other options and let her choose. Always trying to impose your will for the sake of scheduling or expediency is one of the most common and drama-inducing blunders moms make. Conversely, giving your child (some) decision-making authority is only a positive. So why not?

For example, let's say she wants to have an indoor play date with her friend Suzy but it's 75 degrees and sunny outside. Perhaps you negotiate that play date with Suzy for the next rainy day when the two of them are free. Then give her the choice of which park to go to since she didn't get her way, and let her choose what's for lunch that day.

Pay Attention to Health Complaints

It's natural to sometime ignore your daughter's benign complaints. But when she complains about not feeling well, stop what you're doing and investigate. Your first step is to take her temperature (other signs of sickness include sleepiness, headache and a loss of appetite). If you suspect *anything* is wrong, immediately contact your pediatrician, or head directly to an emergency room.

A day after receiving a routine shot, my daughter's arm began to get puffy. I wasn't too concerned about it until the following day when it was red and swollen. My husband took her to the emergency room and learned that she had a serious infection. I should have acted quicker, as fast action is the key to preventing something more serious from happening. And always have your child receive her recommended shots and checkups. That goes for the dentist, too.

On the flip side of this, children will sometimes exaggerate about not feeling well when they don't want to do something, like go to school. (No doubt you can empathize.) Always take your child's complaints seriously but never let her lie about feeling sick. Remind her that it's not a good idea to fake a sickness and tell her all about the boy who cried wolf!

Hold Practice Runs

As we all know, humans are creatures of habit. When I toilet trained my children, one of the things we did was practice getting out of bed and going to the bathroom. I credit those run-throughs for not having accidents in the middle of the night. I also had my children practice feeling the urge to throw up and running to the bathroom. It may sound like overkill, but it's better than cleaning vomit out of a carpet for two hours. You can also use these run-throughs to teach them what to do in case of emergencies like fire or an accident. It's never too early to teach your children about safety.

Don't Party Too Hard

Sadly, going to other children's birthday parties will become a regular part of your life. And as you'll no doubt find out, there's a certain "keeping up with the Jones" aspect to kids' parties. You may feel obliged to invite everyone in your daughter's class to her party, or provide gift bags stuffed with junk. Don't get sucked into the craziness. Only accept invitations to her good friends' parties she wants to attend, and throw the birthday party that fits your style and budget.

These early birthday parties are a good social etiquette teaching moment. Remind your daughter that she won't be invited to every shindig and won't be able to invite everyone to her parties either. I'm always so amazed by how poorly some moms handle these social events—criticizing the venue, complaining about who was and wasn't invited, never sending thank you cards—forgetting that they are sending the wrong messages to their children when drama is unnecessarily created.

KINDERGARTEN

Make Your Children Presentable

There's nothing as awesomely liberating as a pajama jamboree on Saturday morning at home, but when it's time to take your daughter outside, wash her face, comb her hair, put her in clean clothes and wipe her nose throughout the day to keep her looking beautiful. When she starts going to school, this exercise becomes doubly important. Don't fall into the trap of being rushed in the morning. Share a healthful breakfast with her and make sure she looks groomed and nicely dressed before she leaves the house. Besides being a parental obligation, that morning routine will instill a sense of self-respect and dignity in her that will last a lifetime.

This is not to say she should be overly concerned with the way she looks at every moment but children who take pride in their cleanliness and appearance will also give you less of a headache at bath time, when getting ready for school and dressing up for a special occasion.

Foster Imagination

As the saying goes, only boring people get bored. In today's age of non-stop smart-phone stimulation, it's vital that you provide and suggest easy and engaging situations for her to entertain herself, and encourage her creativity whenever you can in big and small ways. Here are a few simple suggestions:

- Sit your child down with blank pieces of paper or a brown paper bag and some markers and an hour will fly by.
- Pull a chair up to the kitchen sink, turn on the water and let her play with metal measure cups, small plastic bowls and plastic bottles to her heart's content. Stay nearby.
- If you're busy and your child is at a loss about what to do, simply tell her that she needs to find something to do herself. (You can give her some helpful hints to get her going.)
- Don't always head to the same playground. My husband's grandfather used to take him and his siblings to cemeteries where they'd make up games based on the names on the tombstones, or he'd bring them to baseball fields, libraries or car dealerships.
- After you read to her, tell your child a different bedtime story every night and have her tell you one, too.
- Why let your child watch a DVD in the car when it has a window? My kids can handle a three-hour drive, no problem. (There are books in the car.)
- When your child is a little older, have her write and act out a little play.
- When you're looking for something to do fold a few pieces of construction paper in half, have your daughter write happy

birthday on the front (each letter in a different color) and leave the inside blank. She can easily fill in the rest the next time you're invited to a birthday party.

Trust Your Instincts

When my oldest daughter was about to leave kindergarten, her teacher suggested repeating kindergarten because she wasn't reading as well as her peers. (Yes, this was kindergarten!) As all new moms will experience firsthand, most parents are obsessed—*obsessed*—with their child's schooling and education. Not me. I care, but I'm not obsessed. I didn't consider for one second having my daughter repeat kindergarten because a) it would have been demoralizing for her, b) she'd lose a lot of her friends and, most important, c) I knew that children learn different things at different speeds.

The amount of hand-wringing moms do over whether to put their child into OT (occupational therapy), or get her a tutor, or have her evaluated for this or that learning disability is akin to the Theater of the Absurd. Yes, some children truly do have special needs, but very often teachers, parents and the system manufacture the confusing drama. Always let common sense, your gut and advice from people you trust guide your decisions. You know your child, and don't let anyone tell you differently. By the end of fourth grade, my daughter had read the entire *Harry Potter* series.

Don't Force Your Kids to Do Anything

Whether it's eating broccoli or taking piano lessons, there are going to be some things your child simply does not want to do. So don't make her! Too many parents don't understand that making their child do something is counterproductive on many levels. For starters, if she refuses to eat broccoli, what's the big deal? Also, it means you're not listening to what she's trying to tell you. And what's more, you're merely teaching a might-makes-right mentality. If your child doesn't want to take soccer lessons, it's okay to try to persuade her. But at a certain point you need to take no for an answer. Because think about it: What adult wants to be forced to do something he or she doesn't want to do? When you find yourself being frustrated with your child, put yourself in her shoes and see if you can't come up with a new approach.

Play Games With Your Child's Head

You may get lucky and never have a strong-willed child who thinks the world revolves around her. But chances are, you're going to hear a resounding "No!" and "I don't want to!" pretty often from your child. What's a parent to do? If you ask your daughter to, say, clean up her mess and she doesn't, then clean up the mess yourself and tell her that you won't be doing something for her the next time she asks. Usually, that reminder is enough, but if it's not, then the next time she wants something—a piece of candy, a toy, you to play a certain game with her—say "no." When she asks why, calmly explain to her that she didn't help you, so you aren't going to do a favor for her. This no-nonsense messaging can be hard to carry out, but it's extremely effective.

Not only does this message teach empathy but it goes a long way for responsibility, too. Children need to learn early on that the world works so much better when we all work together. Like the saying goes, you scratch my back I'll scratch yours. It may be hard for a toddler to comprehend that you, too, are human and have needs (as does dad and big sister) but learning to be empathetic is a necessary part of being a good friend and partner throughout life.

Teach Your Child to Swim

True story: I once attended a wedding and sat next to a wonderful young dad who had a 3-year-old son. A year later, I learned that his boy had recently drowned at a children's birthday party. Every day, about two children drown in the United States, and another 10 receive emergency care for nonfatal submersions. Teach your child how to swim as soon as possible and be unfailingly diligent around pools. Look at it this way: watching your child in a pool for four minutes can seem like forever, while talking to a friend at a pool party for four minutes goes by in the blink of an eye. Just never forget that it takes only four minutes for a child to drown.

Swimming is fun, good exercise, and an activity that most kids will eventually be doing a lot as they get older. Once your child is a strong enough swimmer, it'll benefit her and you. Just think: the sooner she swims safely on her own, the sooner you can accompany her to the pool and read a book while lounging rather than watching her with an unrelenting eagle eye. Not to mention, many summer water sports like tubing, jet skiing, and canoeing require swimming skills, so you may as well prepare her early.

Find Your Child's Talent

Don't you wish you could speak French or Chinese, or play soccer, the piano or chess at an elevated level? I introduced my girls to a myriad of activities to see what would grab hold of their interests and talents and one settled on the guitar, the other on soccer and both love skiing, not surprisingly. Maybe it's sports or painting or ballet or horticulture—but everyone is interested in and good at something. Try to expose your child to as many experiences as possible, and help her stick with it when there's a connection or talent.

Eventually she will find the things that she excels at *and* enjoys. You never know, she may be the next Yo-Yo Ma or Marie Curie. Chances are your child will not want to disappoint you so listen to her clues carefully when assessing whether or not she's sticking with soccer because you played in college or because she really wants to bend it like Beckham.

Teach Thoughtfulness Early

You know people who don't send thank-you notes, who don't call on your birthday, who don't ever make an effort for someone else. Don't let your child (unknowingly) become one of these social underachievers. Always have her make a card for a relative's and friend's birthday, help her send thank-you cards after her birthday party, and let her be a part of the gift buying during the holidays. And even let her donate $10 from her piggybank to her aunt's favorite charity in lieu of a gift to help her understand what giving is really about.

One more important lesson, which has been lost on today's digital-aged kids, is to not let texting or emailing replace snail mail. A hand-written thank-you note emphasizes how thankful you are. Teach your daughter early on about gratitude. By the time she's in high school, it'll be second nature for her to show her appreciation for the little things in life. I'm convinced that being gracious leads to contentment.

Limit Video Games

News flash: it's not appropriate for children—or adults!—to play video games at the dinner table or at restaurants. But of course, everywhere you go, it's all you ever see. Many young, first-time parents may initially subscribe to the noble idea of protecting their child's mind from being mushed by Angry Bird and Minecraft, or, conversely, they may welcome the undeniable babysitting power of iPhones with unabashed vigor. To be clear: there's nothing wrong with kids playing video games, but there's everything wrong with unlimited access to smartphones and video games.

The reason you don't want your child to play games at a restaurant is that it conveys bad manners. It's antisocial and it's just plain lazy parenting. By allowing your child to play at a table, you're actually teaching her how not to become an interesting person capable of carrying on an intelligent conversation. I realize very few six-year-olds can or want to partake in any adult conversation, but they should be sitting there listening politely, coloring on a kid's menu or talking with other children at the table. Some things to keep in mind:

• In my view, a 4- to 10-year-old should be allowed to play video games no more than three times a week for 30 minutes per session. Let them choose the days they get to play.
• Threatening to take away video games is an awesome tool (just be sure to follow through).

• Make sure you know what games your child is playing and let her know she is absolutely not allowed to play any games you don't first okay.

• Give her 10 extra video minutes for good behavior once in a while.

• Don't let video games dominate a play date. Children are meant to play together, not huddle around a three-inch screen for hours on end.

• All video game rules go out the window on airplanes. Time to binge!

AROUND THIRD GRADE

Don't Overschedule

Once your child starts school, you'll soon discover just how many activities there are for children to participate in after school: gymnastics, swimming, soccer, chess, theater, dance basketball—the list goes on forever. You'll have to balance your child's interest in these activities with your instinct about how much is enough. For me, I always like to pick my children up from school three times a week and let them play outside or simply take them home to relax and play.

Crack the Whip

Ever travel to a third-world country? The kids over there grow up fast! Meanwhile too many Americans think it's okay to push their three-year-old around all day in a stroller. Your child will be able to shower by herself, make her bed, get dressed, brush her teeth, comb her hair, set the table, separate laundry, do dishes, dust, rake and do basic chores from an earlier age than you might imagine. And what's more, she will enjoy it. Your job as a mom is to get your child ready to leave you and be self-sufficient, so don't hold her back. You'll be amazed by how much she can and will want to do for herself. The easiest way to introduce chores is via a schedule. Every morning your daughter has to make her bed before breakfast, clear her place at the table after breakfast and then get dressed. Every Saturday morning after cartoons, she has to strip the sheets off her bed and tidy up her room...soon enough she'll be ready to tackle that bathroom.

When you give your child chores, it not only teaches her the importance of helping out the family but it also gives her the confidence she needs to tackle new experiences. There are no mistakes when it comes to making a bed or folding laundry, and practice makes perfect. If you start believing in her abilities at an early age, she'll be the confident college-aged girl who knows how to get things done.

Make Homework a Priority

Parents who like their children to have a lot of homework need to have their heads examined. Numerous studies show that homework offers little aid to a child's overall academic achievement and simply robs children of precious hours of their childhood. Nevertheless, homework is a fact of life and you need to instill good study habits the very first day your child has homework. My routine has been to allow my kids to watch 30 minutes of TV after coming home from school, followed immediately by homework. In my experience, once children know they have to do their homework, it becomes a matter-of-fact process. And stress to them that the harder they work at school, the easier schoolwork will become.

Find a nice quiet spot in the house and have your child sit at that place each time she does her homework. Be sure to have plenty of pencils, erasers, and sharpeners at the ready and don't offer help until she's given her homework a solid try on her own. No child should be struggling with homework. If this becomes a reoccurring pattern for yours, contact your teacher immediately and set up a meeting for the two of you to discuss strategies for improvement. Remember, you are your child's most important advocate at this age and it's vital for you to be involved in all of her school-related triumphs and failures.

Control Your Kids

If you bring your children to someone's home, make sure they behave and mind their manners. Why am I passing on this seemingly obvious bit of advice? You'd be surprised how many parents let their kids run wild, completely oblivious to the fact that the other adults don't appreciate their lack of consideration. And it's imperative that your children say proper hellos, goodbyes and thank-yous to your hosts. Teach this very simple bit of etiquette now and before you know it strangers will be remarking on your child's commendable social graces.

Go Away for the Weekend With Your Husband

Some parents are lucky enough to live near family. If there's someone you trust to take care of your child for a couple of days, take a short vacation with your husband whenever you can. You deserve time to yourselves to keep your relationship happy and healthy. I was unnecessarily worried—bordering on panic—when my husband and I first left our one-year-old with his parents, but she was alive when we got home and overjoyed to see us. I also like to think it taught my daughter that mommy and daddy can go away, but they'll always come back.

A few days alone to re-charge your batteries is always a godsend. Not to mention children love it when grandma and grandpa and aunts and uncles get to spoil them to death.

Talk About Sex

"Having the talk." It's a head-scratcher of a subject many parents don't really want to deal with, but will ultimately have to. The easiest way to take the awkwardness out of this subject is to deal with it as it comes up.

My four-year-old: "Mommy, where do babies come from?"
Me: "You came from my stomach."

My six-year-old: "What is sex?"
Me: "It's when a man puts his penis in a woman's vagina to make a baby."

My nine-year-old: "Mommy, I'm not going to be ready for sex because I don't know how to do it."

Me: "Don't worry. You're not going to have sex until you're much older, and by then you'll know all about it."

If you talk about sex matter-of-factly and your child knows that she can always ask you questions about it, then at least you'll be sure she is getting the proper information. Thanks to the Internet, social media, and reality stars, kids are being exposed to sexualized content earlier than ever. Being the person in your child's life who tells it like it is could ensure later on in life, when things get *really* confusing and serious, that you'll be the one she'll confide in and go to for advice.

Don't Be *That* Mom

True story: my two girls wanted to set up a cookie stand in front of our house with a friend. The three of them made the cookies with my help and then made and decorated the stand. As they were setting up the stand, another girl in the neighborhood, who is typically pushy and rude, said she wanted to help and get an equal part of the money. My girls protested to me in confidence and I told them we'd figure out how to split the money later.

Some 10 minutes after they began selling cookies, the mother of the pushy girl approached the four girls and told them that their goal was to have fun, be safe—they were on the sidewalk—and be fair to each other. As the mother of the girls who came up with the idea, I only wanted to get them out the door and then read a magazine, but this other mom took it upon herself to interject herself in some other children's project for the sake of *her* child. After about two hours, the girls came inside the house, with $24 to show for their efforts. And apparently, another girl joined the group to help hawk the cookies to passersby. So, how to split the money? I gave $6 to each of the three girls who made the cookies and the stand—explaining they were the original partners and did a larger share of the work—and gave the other two girls $3 each. They all happily acknowledged the split was fair, and I sent them back out to clean up.

At that point, the other mother strolled up to the five girls and asked how much money her daughter received—not how much they made, but how much her daughter got. When they told her the breakdown, she sighed and said she *was* going to give the girls a $5 tip to share, but now she was only going to give it to her daughter. What's the lesson this mother taught her daughter? Be rude and pushy and you'll be rewarded with $5.

Get Out of Your Child's Way

With each passing day, your child will be closer to becoming her own person and asserting her independence. Little by little, her life will be more about her, and less about you. Don't fight it. All the clichés hold true: "Let her make her own mistakes;" "Different people want different things;" "It's not for you to decide." As your child starts to identify her own interests and make her own decisions, let her become her own person, not who you think she ought to be. Always remember that the best you can do is give good advice and unswerving support, help out however and whenever you can, set a good example and then stand back and watch. Do that, and you'll be rewarded with a lifetime of love and friendship, as well as some serious entertainment.

HELLO, TWEENS

Sniff Out Any Problems

By now, washing hands, brushing teeth and wearing clean clothes should be perfunctory for your child. It's time to talk about sweat, stinky armpits, body odor, bad breath and the almighty importance of always wearing clean underwear!

Good hygiene promotes good health, too. The moment you smell body odor, introduce deodorant; the moment you smell foot odor, introduce clean socks and a little baking soda into her sneakers in middle school. Children really zone in on the "smelly or dirty" kid and they can be ruthless when it comes to teasing.

Spend Time Alone With Each Child

Being part of a happy and healthy family is not only one of the most rewarding things in life, but spending time together as a family can also promote long-term mental health and stability. As your children grow up, it will become clear that the group dynamic of your family is very different from the one-on-one time both you and your husband share with each of your children. There are a number of reasons why one-on-one time with each child is important and very beneficial.

Besides really getting to know your child, especially a second or third child, spending some one-on-one time with her whenever possible gets the message across that you want to be alone only with her, are interested in her life, her fears, her interests and even her silly side. There's also an extra bonus with one-on-one time: kids are usually much better behaved when a sibling isn't around.

Going on a walk is one of our favorite ways to spend time alone with each of our girls. Whether it's to run errands or just get some fresh air, a walk allows for natural conversations and sharing without any distractions. A ride in the car is also a perfect time and place to start up a conversation that's just between the two of you. Knowing you're confined within four safe doors can provide the vault-like environment she needs to open up and confide.

Make a special arrangement, like going to a movie, with each of your children whenever time, money and energy allow. She'll love you for it and those imperceptible underpinnings of a lifelong friendship will continue to form because you are doing those ordinary things that regular friends do—namely, make time to be together and catch up.

Bedtime is also a treasured time to be together. I am one of those moms who will read to her children for as long as they will let me. Very often, after bonding in this way, an interesting discussion will arise that was prompted by the book's character or plot. Other times we just talk in whispered tones about whatever comes to mind—sometimes I'll ask some probing questions to get things started—and I get to see early glimpses of the person my daughter is growing up to be.

Make the Call on Phones and Privacy

As your child moves into tween territory, some of her more endearing personality traits may fade, giving way to a new sense of independence and self awareness that can be highly irritating. With hormones surging, middle-school friend drama brewing and pre-pubescent angst rearing its unruly head, there will be no more important time to set the stage for communication. Tweens are by nature moody know-it-alls, trying your patience on a daily basis. But remember: this time can also be a lonely and confusing one for your child. Luckily, you've been letting them know for years that you're available, without (too much) fear of consequence or judgment, should they need help. Initiating important conversations will remind your child that you care about her and her well-being.

Asking about her friends, her activities, and even her fears won't always precipitate an open and honest discussion, but don't stop trying. Once, when I suspected my daughter was having a major argument with her best friend, I began our conversation by bringing up some of the awkward times I went through in middle school. I imagined she'd realize that instead of trying to pry, I was sharing so the two of us could get to know more about one another.

Surveillance (aka spying) is another simple way to discover what's going on in your tween's life. Children these days get phones starting in fourth, fifth or sixth grade, and they are virtual diaries, as well as instruments of amusements and destruction. The age you decide to give your child a phone, apps and certain Internet access is your call, but here are a few suggestions.

I didn't let either of my children have a phone (old iPhones) until the beginning of sixth grade, even though many of their friends had phones a year or two earlier. And despite all of their friends being allowed to have various social media accounts like Facebook and Instagram, I didn't allow them until they were 13. I remember when my eldest was 11 and some of my mom friends caved on giving their 10- and 11-year-olds access to social media, justifying it by saying they planned to monitor the account, with their child's knowledge, every day. Fast forward a year or two, and I can't tell you how many dinners I've had with these same moms where the conversation was dominated by how social media was disrupting their children's lives in the most unhealthy way: obsession with being popular, bullying, getting in trouble at school, developing body issues, losing interest in schoolwork...you name it. By contrast, I just explained to my somewhat annoyed daughter that she'd have to wait until she was 13 to get a social media account, and we both avoided years' worth of drama. (More about social media in a couple of pages.)

When we did give my daughter her first phone, the rules were simple:

• The primary reason for having a phone is to communicate with mom and dad.

• No Internet access, just phone, texting and email. (At age 12 we allowed *restricted* Internet access.)

• We knew the password and randomly checked the phone. We'd check the phone only once or twice a week and accepted that she was old enough to keep certain things about her relationships private.

• No earphones or music services, lest she be distracted while walking across a street or riding on her bike.

• Once home from school, phones get put away for the night, save for five or 10 minutes to return any text messages from friends.

Continue to Help With Homework

As your child advances through elementary school, homework will continue to become a more important and, perhaps, more arduous part of her everyday life. My children always do homework at the kitchen table, usually while I am preparing dinner. This way, we're all busy working and I am on hand for support, but not hovering.

As I've mentioned, it's a good practice for children to always attempt to complete homework on their own. Certainly, I've helped my daughters with their homework, but giving them the self-confidence to do homework on their own is as important as the homework itself. Once the homework is complete, check it. For my eldest daughter, my husband or I spot-checked every night until she was finished with eighth grade and had finally become a fully self-sufficient student. I stopped checking my younger daughter's homework in sixth grade because she was very serious and all business when it came to homework, so the training wheels came off early. And for both children, I hired tutors on a couple of brief occasions to help prepare for important state tests.

Another aspect of schoolwork that requires eternal vigilance is reading. Even if your child isn't given a reading assignment every evening, the most productive activity any child can do to keep up with schoolwork is to read. Be involved in helping her choose books and let her choose what she wants. No one ever became an avid reader by having someone force books into their hands.

And again, if your child ever starts to struggle with the amount or difficulty of her homework, or anything else related to school, act quickly! Contact the teachers, get a tutor if needed, double-check her homework and correct it together—do whatever is necessary to get over the hump so she doesn't get discouraged and fall behind or run into further difficulty.

Monitor Social Media

By the time your child hits 10-years-old, she will already be asking about social media. The most popular apps out there for kids today are Instagram, Kik and Snapchat among others, many of which are used for their ability to hide the user's identity and activity. There really aren't any golden rules when it comes to social media My husband and I didn't let our children use any social media whatsoever until they reached 13.

There are a number of reasons that this family rule felt right to us. The first is that neither of us uses social media, not that we don't get the appeal. Second is that app developers themselves recommend that kids under 13 years of age don't download their product. But the main reason was the insane amount of pressure we got from our children to allow them to have social media, which I thought was an indication of the insane amount of time and drama that social media invites. I know moms whose worlds have risen and crashed because of social media, so I couldn't imagine—and refused to allow—the drama it would surely have had on my own kids.

Social media complicates things. It confuses friendships, prizes popularity and invites bullying. Everyone knows that kids can be mean, and that goes double when they can taunt through a faceless app. It's bad enough that a boy or girl might get bullied at school or on the bus ride home, but these days many tormented children aren't even safe within the four walls of their own bedroom.

Holding out on social media for tweens/teens as long as possible will pay off in the end. Your child will have no other choice but to live in the moment and hone their actual—real— social skills. When your child hits 13, ask her if she wants to partake in social media and, if she does, have her choose an app. Let her know you'll be monitoring what she posts so remind her not to put anything out there that she doesn't want mom and dad to know about. Also, be crystal clear about the consequences of posting something that could a) get them in serious trouble and b) very well live on the Internet forever. College admission offices check the social media accounts of perspective students and today's human resources departments definitely look at social media accounts to determine the character of a job applicant. To help reinforce the ramifications of bad judgment on social media, I relate cautionary tales from the news to my daughters all the time.

Keep This Book Handy

I'm well aware that none of the information in this book is groundbreaking. After all, most of it came from my reading other books and articles and speaking to countless other mothers about their experiences. And while I wrote *The Modern Mother's Handbook* so it could be read in about 60 minutes, carrying out its recommendations will take years of dutiful resolve, patience and sacrifice. Teach your child to go to sleep. Teach your child to swim. Teach her to eat healthy food and how to love to read. Those aren't options and they don't come easy. Teach your child manners. Teach her to express herself, to do well in school and to understand how to make smart decisions. Of course, all of those decisions ultimately start with you—the first one being, what kind of mom are you going to be?

Printed in Great Britain
by Amazon